KALEIDOSCOPE
OF LOVE

also by K.J. Robinson
Conversations with The Universe

KALEIDOSCOPE
OF LOVE

Kaleidoscope of Love Copyright © 2023 by Kim Joanna Robinson.

Book Cover Design by R. Clift. rcliftpoetry.com
Book Interior Design and Layout by K. J. Robinson
Edited by Shelby Leigh

First printing edition, 2023.

ISBN: 978-3-9825444-0-3

To the person who taught me
that love doesn't end with saying goodbye.
To the person who showed me
that love endures pain.
To the person who proved
that healthy love still exists.

Thank you for opening up my eyes.
Thank you for showing me
that love is a rainbow
with many different colors.

CONTENTS

INTRODUCTION

DEAR READER,

Love is one of the most complex and mysterious emotions that
we experience in our lives. It can be seen from many different
angles and it can look vastly different from one moment to the
next.

This collection of poetry intends to explore all aspects of
love—how it can change and shift like a kaleidoscope, and
how love doesn't end with saying goodbye.

Whether it's romantic or platonic love, this book explores the
light and dark sides of relationships, capturing the range of
emotions that come with loving another person: from pain and
sadness to excitement and exhilaration.

Thank you for giving these words a home,

KJ

ROSE-COLORED GLASSES

Love,
the universal language.
It's always with you,
always there,
so very real.

Not to see
with physical senses,
but to deeply feel,
if you only let down
your defenses.

IN MY DREAMS

I met my soulmate in my dreams last night.
I knew, because their energy felt familiar.

A familiar energy filling my heart, I knew
without realizing, this person I will one day meet.

I will meet this person one day, without understanding
the where, the what, the who, the when.

When, where, who, what—none of it really matters.
The energy will guide me to them, as if by magic.

Magically, I shall be guided by their energy.
Kill all doubts, no more worry and panic.

No more room for my panic, worry and doubts,
and in a flash, I can feel that hope again.

I can feel hopeful again because in a flash,
I met my soulmate in my dreams last night.

And I don't yet know
who you are,
but I know
my heart's
longing for you.

And for some
this may sound bizarre,
but I know
when we meet,
we will both realize
we are
each other's
counterpart.

Soulmates
are people
who enter your life
and supposedly
it's by fate.
I don't know about
the universe's workings;
all I can say,
all I do know,
is that those are people
with whom I instantly
resonate
and for whom my soul
willingly waits.

I don't date
because I got scared of diving
into the dark.

I got tired of being the bait
of the trials and tribulations
of finding a starfish among the swarms
and dangers and endless vastness
which will surely leave me marked.

I don't date
because I am afraid
of swimming with sharks.

But I do fate
because I believe to find true love
I won't have to endure the dark;
I know a starfish
can also be found on the beach,
on a walk.

I wish
for lighthearted times
and a love so divine
that I don't have to
read between the lines.

I Want a Quiet, Calm Love

The kind that comes
when you're not seeking
and suddenly someone shows you
the smallest of gestures
that make the biggest impact.

The kind that comes
when you're not trying
or thinking
of what to say—
you're just being you
and that's enough
in each and every way.

ETERNAL HEARTS

Two eternal hearts
made to find each other
again and again,
story after story.
The circumstances
keep shifting
but not the love that exists
for another;
different faces,
different places,
waiting for their love
to be rediscovered.

I want to love,
let the past be the past,
give true love the chance
to last.

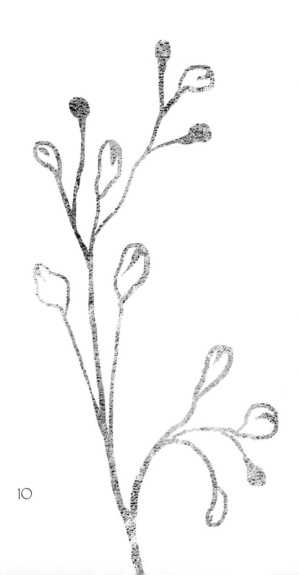

ENERGETIC BOND

It seems like
time is standing still,
in these moments
I can feel your energy close by,
even though far away
I can sense your smile;
in these moments
I forget to wonder
how much longer until
we meet—
knowing for you,
it'll be worth the wait.

YOU CAN HEAL IT
BUT YOU CAN ALSO
BREAK IT APART.
PLEASE, BE GENTLE
WITH MY HEART.

When you know,
without a doubt,
that they are the one
you've been waiting for—
someone who will always be there,
always with you—
the one who will never let you down,
see you for who you really are:

it's like the stars align
and you've never felt so alive.

THINGS I WANT

A place to live
the one that my heart calls me to
where I have space to walk and hike
and feel like I belong.
The place that makes me feel
like I finally arrived.

A house with a view
one that instantly sparks affection
where I can be close to nature
the one I always dreamed of
not just a building to survive.

I want
a place to come home to
a special connection
where I feel like
I'm being wrapped up in your love
where every day my feelings renew
and everything is true
in that beautiful place
of me and you.

Love me
beneath
a thousand stars.
Love me
despite
all of my scars.

If you want to love me
you have to
love me whole.
'Cause I'm done
bending and pretending.

—*I'm an all-or-nothing soul.*

Your energy
feels familiar
like it has always been
me and you.
Like we met
throughout many
lifetimes.
Like we were guided
to each other
again and again
by love streaming
beneath our feet.

—*Can you feel it, too?*

Aren't we all a little bit broken
in a way?
And aren't we all looking for healing
each and every day?
And isn't it beautiful
when two souls meet
and they each have
what the other needs?
And doesn't all the past hurt
feel worth it
because you met them
and can witness
how the circle completes?

And when
I first saw your name,
the world stopped around me.
In my mind
a symphony played—
the universe's clue.
A voice inside me saying:
it's you.

I look at you
and wonder:

Where were you
all this time?
Where did
the universe hide you?
How is it
that my life changed
in an instant
and turned into
all I ever asked for?
And how can someone
with such a pure soul
like yours even exist
in the same world
that shattered me
to pieces?
And yet here you are
choosing me regardless—

I look at you
and wonder:
are you real?

I just think and dream
of everything about you.
The smile on your face,
appreciating all of the beauty
I so easily find in you.

And should there ever be a time
where you're not feeling your best,
I just want to be there,
holding you close to my chest.

THE POTION OF LOVE

From blue skies
and deep oceans
between us,
love is the potion
that helps us rise.

Distance means so little;
it hardly bears in mind
when two hearts
are vibrationally aligned.

Nothing could keep us
from finding each other.
Adventure is calling
for a world to discover.

MY HEART LONGS
FOR YOURS,
KNOWING YOUR HEART
ALSO LONGS FOR MINE.

I CAN FEEL US WALKING
ON THE SAME PATH,
SO DIVINE.

I want to be the first
to capture all of your beauty—
the perfect imperfections—
yes, even what others
might view as flaws.
Wrap my love into countless poems
for you—
so that you may know it,
too.

27

If my heart could speak
it would tell it like it is, everytime.
The truth that love seeks.

Do you even notice
how you're slowly picking up
the pieces of me that got
S H A T T E R E D
in my past,
how you're putting me back
T O G E T H E R
with your words,
with your gestures,
with your reassuring touch?

It's just you being you
but you're better
than anyone I could have
ever asked.

Our love
cannot be diminished.
The only thing it does is
E X P A N D .
So let me hold
both your hands
for I know
with absolute certainty
this love only knows
how to
WITHSTAND.

I want your arms
wrapped around me tight,
never letting go,
that would feel so right.

Your love and mine,
UNIFIED,
we radiate
a golden glow of light.

I feel your energy.
Everything around me
falling away,
fading out of view.

I sense your presence
and it grounds me
in such a gentle way.
Can you feel it, too?

Of all the things
I wished for
your name
wasn't even on my list;
still, it made everything
fall short
the moment
that we kissed.

I reach
for your
gentle touch.
Still feel
your hand
around mine.
An energy
so divine.

Thoughts of you
keep me awake
at night,
a constant replay
inside my mind.

I give in.
I no longer want to fight.

These words
that you speak—
it's like
you somehow know
I need them—
the reassurance
the affirmations
the compliments.
They are soothing
and calming
and slowly healing
my soul.

Please, don't let them be
just a phase.
Please, never stop,
not even after
thousands of days.

I want to erase
all past memories
of people and places
of hurt and pain
and past nightmares.
I want to replace them
with thoughts of you
with vacations
and day trips
with funny moments
and inside jokes.
I want to create
brand new memories
of us talking
of us dancing
of us late-night driving
and romantic sunset walking.

And I hope you want that, too.

YOUR KISS.
YOUR HUG.
YOUR EYES ON MINE.
AND I FEEL YOU
FROM ACROSS THE ROOM—
ELECTRIC CRUSH.

I wake up
and I think of you.
I see the sun
and I think of you.
I have fun
and I think of you.
I go for a drive, feeling free,
and I think of you.
I drink tea at five
and I think of you.
I look at the moon
and I think of you.
I hear my favorite tune
and I think of you.
I cuddle my dog
and I think of you.

Yes, I could keep a log
with hundreds of pages,
yet still, keep a hundred more
thoughts of you in q u e u e .

There's no one quite like you,
no one else I want to turn to.
A magical aura surrounding
your whole being;
an energy

so grounding,

I suddenly know exactly
what I am seeking—

you.

43

Never
have I been
the lucky one
who was allowed
to ask for
or receive
reassurance
from another
but it all changed
with you—
the one
who freely gives.

I'm proud to be
your lover.

YOU ARE LOVE

right to your core.
An aura
so enticing
it leaves me
wanting more.

YOU ARE LOVE

so pure
it is all
I have ever
asked for.

Can you hear
my heart?
It's singing, oh so loud.
A sound made only
for your ears.
No one else allowed.

My love reaches out
LIKE WAVES
crashing into the seaside,
again and again.
I'LL NEVER GROW TIRED,
of swimming by your side,
for without loving you,
everything turns into
SHADES OF BLUE.

I feel safe here.

But here
isn't a place.
It's wherever I am with you.

HOW I FEEL WHEN I THINK OF YOU

I'm in a field of sunflowers,
feels like I have higher powers.
The world turns upside down,
my lips never in a frown.
Colors around me get much brighter;
my whole being feels lighter.
An urge to sing and dance;
every moment
becomes a brand-new chance.

AND WITH
EVERY SECOND
THAT PASSES
I ONLY SEE
CHANCES TO
LOVE YOU MORE.

And only now have I realized
that all this time I was drowning
until you reached out your hand—
I'm so glad I took it.
Because for the first time in my life
I know what it's like
to be able to breathe
without *gasping* for air.

You stopped when you saw me
and offered your hand—
I'm still holding it
and I'm not letting go.

I need you,
and you need me.
That's all that matters—
to feel, to understand.
I know you're afraid,
and I'm scared, too.
But when you need me,
I'll always be there
for you.

I WAS DROWNING
UNTIL MY LOVE
FOR YOU
OVERFLOWED
THE ENTIRE UNIVERSE,
AND LIFTED MY HEAD
ABOVE WATER.

You are a
KALEIDOSCOPE OF LOVE,
showing me all different lenses
what healthy love is supposed
to be; there's no need for
past defenses and
FEELING SAFE
is the only
thing I
feel.

Hold my hand.
DANCE WITH ME
through the night.
There's no end,
TOGETHER
and always close by—
you and me.
Please never say
GOODBYE.

TWISTS
AND
TURNS

„I'm sorry" —

such simple words
carrying
so much meaning.

Not easy
to say
but important
to find.

„I'm sorry" —

for messing up.
Sometimes
I just lose
my mind
and get lost.

"I'm sorry" —

will we
be able
to forgive,
forget
and rewind?

PROMISE ME

You introduced me to your broken world
but you didn't want me in it.
You thought I didn't belong because I looked innocent, clean.
You didn't want to drag me into it. I could see it in your eyes.
How you felt every time I stepped deeper into your life.
Like taking a beautiful piece of art and pouring black paint over it.
Like cutting off an angel's wings. But on the other side of things,
being with each other got us high and so
we were bound to cross some lines.
You crossed mine many times, but I kept returning.
I tried to understand why.
For a long time, I didn't find the answer.
Then I realized that you are the answer.

So promise me I'll see your face when I get high—
it was you who introduced me to this world anyways.

POLARITY OF LOVE

I once wondered,
what does true love mean?
How long I must've pondered,
is it only thought of with ease?

My conclusion: no.
For life contains
both light and shadow.

It's yin and yang,
not one without the other.
That's how you can truly
love one another.

SECRET THOUGHTS

I just left
but already
I am
missing you.
Now I'm
sitting here
wondering,
do you feel
the same
about me,
too?

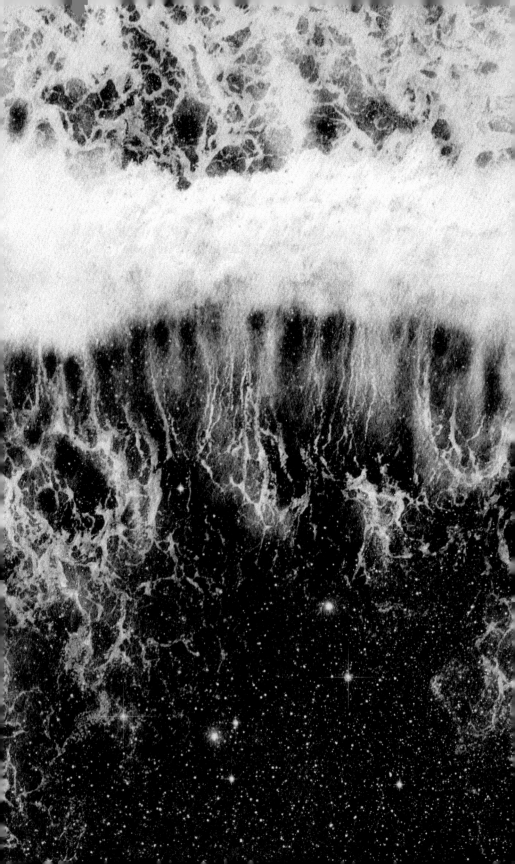

I would give up everything,
even travel across
the ocean for you
Yes, I would do anything,
if you'd let me know,
that you want me to.

Yes, I'm being truthful here,
this being the full scope
of what you truly mean to me.

—*For me you are a world of hope.*

FACETS OF LOVE

For me, love is true
when it consists of all facets
that life has to offer.

You are bound to suffer
if you dismiss
the beauty that can be found
in both light and dark.

I want it too,
but
my mind
is in the way.
First,
I need to hear you say
you are the one,
the only one for me,
my future—
the kind of devotion
that makes people
pray.

HIDDEN MESSAGE

I received a mystery.
Through a passage
I retrieved
its meaning.

All this time
I was holding my breath
how good it felt
when I finally
breathed.

Or was it just
a sneeze
because just as quick
it was gone
and I don't know
if I should still believe.

I want you so much
that it feels a little too much.
My emotions are running
in such extremes
that love
passion
trust
and craving
your gentle touch
all radiate from me in beams.

Is it safe
to feel this much?

THOUGHTS I TRY TO HIDE

The endless doubts and worries
that keep on spinning inside my head,
trying to decipher your messages
and what it is you really meant;

the question of whether I've lost my mind;
if so, it must have been a while ago,
and whether your awareness even
includes my existence—
sometimes I can't tell truth from fiction
and really don't know;

the fact that I feel invisible
compared to your entourage
while simultaneously wondering
whether your social picture is real
or just camouflage;

the things I wanted to ask you
since day one:

Does it matter?
Do you feel it too?
Is this love real?
Or was it just
some grand mirage?

Did I do it again?
Did I mess things up
between us?
Did I say too much?
Did I make you run
by being my true self
too soon?

I guess I am too intense;
I can understand
it's too much fuss.
Who would like a girl
as such?
Too afraid to know the truth,
so instead
I will ask the moon.

I'm scared
of going deep
into the forest
while you stay close
to the outskirts
to keep the road in sight.
I have this fear
that soon
you'll be taking flight
and I'll
fall into
a rabbit hole again
where I feel anything
but alright.

Are you
gonna love me
just to throw
me away?
Or are you
gonna love me
and stay?

You caught my eye and
yes, you stole my heart.

So tell me—your plan—
was it to be just another guest
that sells it to the next thief
or to be the future owner
and never leave?

If I'm being honest,
I would much more prefer
for you to be by my side
when making the transfer
to the next phase of our lives,
than to be all on my own.
I know, now it's up to you to decide—
will you pick up the phone,
give love a try?

I fall too fast
and too soon.
I fall all at once
just like the stars do
every night
when they see the moon.

A little birdie told me
you're still thinking about me
and that you're out there
waiting for a sign.

Well, I'm here.
I still think about the good old days.
I miss our inside jokes
and our secret back-and-forths
because your energy pulls me in
like a compass pointing
true north.

Standing here
at this open door,
waiting with patience
for some time more.
Hoping you might still come,
I need you to know,
there's still time left to join.

Today
I don't cry
out of sadness.
No, I cry
because my love
for you is so strong
that I know
it will be lifelong.

IN-BETWEEN

We are somewhere between lovers and friends
but the lines got blurry along the way
and I lost track of any sort of definition that could bring us justice.
But what if we're right where we're supposed to be
—for each other an in-between?

And believe me
when I say
I'd go on this ride
with you again,
in the blink of an eye.
'Cause love
is what I'm made of
and I will wait for you
to come along.

So many reminders,
they just won't stop.
The universe
must be conspiring
against me.
Your name is still
everywhere I go,
and I ask myself,
did I make the
right decision
by letting you go?

DARK
REFLECTIONS

IT'S STILL LOVE

if after months of back and forth
you choose to get up and leave.
If the very thought of them
breaks your heart
into a million little pieces,
but still you go,
because you not only love them,
you also love yourself,
and over time you learned
that some people need to be loved
from a distance,
if it means
not losing yourself.

What I would do
to have you close
to reach for your scent—
of that I certainly
dreamt.

What I would do
to tell you all
that I really meant—
the thought alone
leaving me more
content.

What I would do
is leave out
the resentment,
and you leaving
I would prevent.

But you left
and took
those dreams
I never dreamt.

THE I-MISS-YOU-LIST

You asked me for
my bucket list,
so I wrote one.
Did you know
each item
once included you?
But now,
we no longer exist
and to do them
without you,
I want to resist.

I tried to
replace you
with him.
I wanted to
convince myself
that it felt safe
that it felt right.
Logic told me
to love him
is the right thing
to do

— but he is not you.

And I still
long to reach out to you
to hear your voice
just one more time.
To feel your arms around me.
But then
the memories come back
and I remember
why I left.

SUSPENDED STORY

Things ended
way too suddenly,
feels like
our story
got suspended;
losing you,
my greatest defeat,
wishing our differences
I would have amended,
but maybe
in a different life
our love will repeat;
then,
newly united,
we can make
our story complete.

And I guess
you got scared of losing me—
not because I gave you a reason to,
but because your past
left you scarred.

UNANSWERED QUESTIONS

Why didn't you come in sooner
with your apologies?
Why did you wait
to tell me you love me?
Why did you make me
want to chase you
and ignore you
at the same time?

Maybe sometimes
the purpose of a love story
is to end
in the most dramatic
and heart-wrenching way
so that the pain
inspires you to finally
heal yourself.

I'm sorry
we didn't work out.
We both saw the potential
for a beautiful future
but I guess
the universe
had different plans.

All these times
I contemplated
getting in the car
and driving to your place.
The happy memories come
rushing in
and I smile before
they fade.
The reason I never came
was the memories
that haunted me—
they still do.

Why do I
still miss you
after everything that happened?
Why is everything
I feel for you love?

— *I expected hurt and sadness.*

CONFESSION

You know, I really did love you
and it hurt when you acted like I didn't.

You acted like I didn't and that hurt
so much that it made me love you less.

I thought that it made me love you less,
but it didn't because feeling hurt means you love someone.

It means you love someone if you feel this much hurt.
It also means they aren't able to love you right.

If they aren't able to love you right,
it means they don't even love themselves.

When I realized you didn't love yourself,
I realized that things would never change.

You'd never change, so I left and it still hurts because
you know, *I really did love you.*

REMINDERS OF YOU

The brand of your car.
The one song you played on repeat.
The smoke of cigarettes.
The places we claimed as our own.
The shows we watched on tv.
The kisses we shared.
The sunsets we saw.
The dreams we had.
The sadness hiding behind your eyes.

These things
will forever
remind me of you.

You've really
had it going for you,
but you didn't notice,
too busy,
trying to make me jump
through your hoops
and so
you took our love
and crushed it.

And they take
everything
from you
until you can't even
breathe.
But still, it's not
enough.
They keep taking
until
there is nothing

      left

          of

              y

                o

                  u

                   ...

They say they'll change,
but they never do.
The same promises
they have always made,
and they still won't change.

It's always the same story,
same excuses and lies.
They say they'll change,
but they never do.

Shouting your pain at me
did nothing but push me
FURTHER AWAY.
Your screams only made me feel
MORE ALONE
and I couldn't bear
to see you suffer anymore.
So I turned my back and
WALKED AWAY.

IT WAS MY CHOICE
TO LEAVE
BUT THEN AGAIN
YOU DIDN'T EXACTLY
LEAVE ME
ANY OTHER OPTION.

WHY YOU TRY

You do your best.
You buy them flowers.
You take them out,
then they tell you
it's not enough.

So you try even more.
You give your all
yet they don't see it.
All you get are breadcrumbs,
question marks inside your head
and unrealistic demands.

Still, you keep going.
You tell yourself it will be worth it,
while you completely dismiss
your own needs,
dreams and wishes.
Until you reach the point
where you can't even say

why
you still try

why
the thought of leaving them
still makes you ache

but deep down you know
this thing
—it will break.

I stayed too long and left the moment I realized
you were just making me feel worse in the end.
I should've known it would come to this.
And now I'm paying for my mistake.
I should've just walked away
— *but I wanted to believe that things could change.*

POLARITY

When I close my eyes,
you're no longer there, haunting
me inside my dreams.

I still dream of you.
It's as if you never left
when I close my eyes.

Didn't you notice
my feelings,
like, for real,
or did you
confuse me
on purpose?

I will never forget
your smile
and your free laughter,
how you held my hand
and told me stories that let me wonder
how brave you must have been.

But I also will never forget
the way you first screamed at me
and went cold,
how you pushed me away
with your cruel words
and didn't let me back in,
how I tried to stay and help
but whatever I did,
it was never right.

I will never forget
the moment I decided to leave—
not because I didn't care,
but because I cared too much.

The seasons will change,
the moon will wax and wane,
but they WON'T CHANGE.
They'll always be THE SAME.

Unchanging, unyielding,
never learning from their mistakes
THEY'LL NEVER CHANGE.
The cycle of pain and suffering
will continue until the end of time,
because they WILL NEVER
make up THEIR MIND.

FALSE CHANCES

Your friends used to
make fun of you
for giving me
too many chances
and you got angry
when you noticed
it wasn't you
who extended the chances—
it was me.

They will never hear you out.
To them, you're just a speck
of dirt on the windshield.
A voice that can be drowned out
by their own rhetoric.

Accept it and leave.
Your words won't ever change their mind.
Walk away from the fight.
Find someone who will listen.

YOU CAPTURED MY HEART
BUT ACTED AS IF
YOU STILL HAD TO GAIN IT.

The moments
I can only remember
THE GOOD PARTS
these are my
FAVORITE MOMENTS.

I still think of you
during the day
when I am reminded
of something we once
did together,
a place we used to go to,
the restaurants we went to
and the things we laughed about.

I still think of you
and I think
it will always be this way.

TO HEAL A TRAUMATIZED HEART

spend some time alone and prioritize yourself. Fall back in love with yourself. Treat yourself. Care for yourself. Let all the hurt and pain of the past spill out. Take a drive in nature. Stop to cry and scream as much as you need to. Sit with your feelings and don't push them down. Go for a hike in the forest. Move your body. Stretch it out.

Write down all your thoughts and burn the paper afterwards. Throw away anything that reminds you of them. Don't go back and think you could have saved them. Stop taking on feelings of guilt, that you could have tried harder. Realize that you did the best you could. Talk about it with a friend or a loved one.

Don't close off your heart to new love. Find a healthy relationship that teaches you what love really means. Find someone who loves you in your happy and your sad moments. Don't hold back your past trauma and insecurities; talk about them with someone you confide in.

Find someone who wants you to tell them what you need and then delivers. Find someone who makes it feel safe to be yourself. Find someone with whom it's an equal give and take. Trust that this person is out there for you. Never lose hope. Don't assume that in order to find them, you have to be fully healed from your past. Nothing in life is perfect. They will love you, not regardless of your trauma, but even more so for it. Because it makes you real. So don't turn cold and distant, but stay soft and vulnerable

— *it's your gift.*

Our time was short
but still
I don't resent
meeting you.
Quite the contrary—

I thank you
for opening up
my eyes.

HOPING FOR THAT ONE DAY

Your old cigarette lighter is still sitting on my desk,
in the same spot since we last talked.
I haven't moved it or touched it
even after months and months of silence.

Every time I see it I have to think of you.
Then I wonder how something can look
so unapologetic, yet at the same time hold the potential
to destroy forests and houses
with just one single, uncareful spark.

I look at it and am reminded
of the look on your face whenever you lit up
another cigarette. How your muscles tensed,
how everything around you vanished in smoke,
how every color turned black, how the life in you
went out, how your sadness resurrected and how your eyes
went hollow.

I now look at the same lighter
and wonder how something once filled
with such power and potential could become
this empty and filled with sorrow.

Every time I look at it, I flash back and see you.

And I keep looking at it, every day
because I can't give up on the thought
that one day its liquid might magically return.
The universe's way of telling me
that yours has, too.

And I guess
THINGS HAVE CHANGED
as the future that once
was spread out before us
VANISHED
in seconds.
At first I thought
I was going insane
but now I see
it's better when we walk
ON DIFFERENT LANES.

I got tired of waiting
for you to come around.
I got tired of waiting
for you to finally see me.
I got tired of waiting
for your love to shine down on me.
I got tired of waiting
so I decided to move on.
I got tired of waiting
for you to change your mind.
I got tired of waiting
for you to come back to me.
I got tired of waiting

—*so I started living my life.*

I was trying
so hard to make you mine;
all the synchronicities
I thought the universe aligned
but it turned out
they weren't hints
for a future
of you and me
side by side.

Now
I can see them
through different eyes—
now
I let them all just be a sign
that the universe is
nearby.

TEN OUT OF TEN

You weren't
my ten out of ten
but I liked
the thought of you
so I didn't care
back then.

I thought
not getting all I wanted
was okay;
I thought
you were close enough,
so please stay.

But it didn't work out
and you left;
now I know
my inner voice
was guiding me
along the way
and never will I
mistrust it again.

Thank you
for opening up my eyes.
Thank you
for bringing me back to life.

Our love didn't last
but still,
it was more
than a short time.
Within my heart
you will live forever.
Etched into poetry,
rhyme by rhyme,
line by line.

WISHES TO AN OLD LOVER

And I hope
you're doing well.
Not too much
hiding
inside your shell.
I hope you will get
yourself some help
and finally learn
to love yourself.

Thank you, dear reader,
for giving this book a home.
For choosing love and
welcoming it into your heart.

And remember, that love is not
always easy, but it is always worth
fighting for. It is a force that can heal
even the deepest wounds and
bring light to the darkest corners
of our hearts.

Ingram Content Group UK Ltd.
Milton Keynes UK
UKHW020812060623
422954UK00016B/1080